Fashion, Power, Guilt

Carol Shields is one of Canada's most acclaimed writers, and is the recipient of, most recently, the Pulitzer Prize for literature, the National Book Critics Circle Award, and the Governor General's Award for *The Stone Diaries*. Her eight novels (which also include *Happenstance* and *The Republic of Love*), two collections of short stories, three volumes of poetry, and five plays (including *Thirteen Hands* and *Departures and Arrivals*, both published by Blizzard), have been among North America's best received writing in recent years. Some of her works are set in Winnipeg, where she has lived for nearly two decades, and where she teaches at the University of Manitoba.

Catherine Shields grew up in the kind of home where those who waited to speak were never heard, where stories were related at great speed, and where exaggeration was encouraged. She has worked as a researcher for UNESCO, and is presently Librarian and Archivist for the Winnipeg Art Gallery. Catherine Shields collaborated on both *Thirteen Hands* and *Departures and Arrivals*.

FASHION, POWER, GUILT
AND THE CHARITY OF FAMILIES

Blizzard Publishing • Winnipeg

Fashion, Power, Guilt, and the Charity of Families
first published 1995 by
Blizzard Publishing Inc.
73 Furby Street, Winnipeg,
Canada R3C 2A2
© 1993 Carol Shields and Catherine Shields

Cover art by Michael Boss.
Printed in Canada by Friesen Printers.

Published with the assistance of
the Canada Council and the Manitoba Arts Council.

Caution

Canadian Cataloguing in Publication Data

Shields, Carol,   1935-
    Thirteen Hands
    A play.
    ISBN 0-921368-59-3
I. Shields, Catherine, 1962-   II.Title
PS8587.H46F3 1995   C812'.54   C95-920181-5
PR9199.3.S44F3 1995

To our families.

Fashion, Power, Guilt, and the Charity of Families was first produced at The Prairie Theatre Exchange in Winnipeg on March 9, 1995 with the following cast:

SALLY	Sarah Neville
MOTHER/WOMAN	Jan Skene
FATHER/MAN ONE	Robb Paterson
MICHAEL	Leigh Rivenbark
CHARACTER #5	Robert Vezina

Director: Micheline Chevrier
Assistant Director: Maggie Nagel
Set and Costume Designer: Jennifer Cooke
Lighting Designer: Kevin Lamotte
Composer / Musical Director: Cathy Nosaty
Stage Manager: Katie R. East
Assistant Stage Manager: Russell Martin
Stage Management Intern: Arlo C. Bates

Playwrights' Notes

Family is the most universal of our institutions, and the most mysterious and private in its workings. It seemed important to question the basic assumptions about the nuclear family by placing abstract commentary margin-to-margin with the ongoing life of a "real" family, and bringing music and drama edge-to-edge in order to open that question as far as it would allow.

Carol Shields

I am fascinated by the power behind the drive we all share to find or create some kind of family (whatever form this may take: two people, or a commune). Yet the desire to escape the fury of family is just as strong. What's the deal here?

Catherine Shields

These are the ideas that brought us to the beginning of our play.

Production Notes

Fashion, Power, Guilt, and the Charity of Families is episodic in form, consisting of a number of vignettes that seek to question the conventional notion of the nuclear family. While not a musical, the play includes several song numbers and uses music as a connection between scenes. The tone of the play varies from the surreal to the sharply realistic, and it is hoped that lighting will enhance these shifts.

The play uses "the house" as motif and setting. There is a living room and kitchen on the first level. At the back of the kitchen is a door to the outside, and beside it is a row of four hooks for coats. At centre stage is a large fridge which masks the access to the second storey. Upstairs there are two small bedrooms.

The five actors are: a father, a mother, a son (12), a daughter (15), and a fifth character (male or female) who plays a variety of roles, including MAN TWO, REAL ESTATE AGENT, CONSULTANT, NEWSPAPER CARRIER, and BABY CARRIER.

Act One

Scene One

(The stage is a dark and vacant house. MAN TWO enters. He wears a black overcoat and carries a black briefcase. Pausing in the kitchen, he strikes a match loudly with a flash of light, and lights a lantern. A soft light fills only the kitchen area of the set. It is obvious that the house has been unoccupied and unheated for some time. He keeps his coat on and sits at the kitchen table.)

MAN TWO: Dear Sir or Madam. I have a complaint which I wish to draw to your attention. Your ... immediate attention. Despite the rising economy ... despite the network of ... hmm ... social programs ... despite the free library lectures ... despite the universal clothing allotment ... not that I'm ungrateful *(Pats his jacket approvingly.)* ... Despite a postal service second to none ... despite the availability of high quality television programming ... and here I wish to congratulate you, dear sir or madam ... despite your unquestionable good will ... I find myself ... I find myself ... I find myself ... extremely ... lonely. L-o-n-e-l-y. *(He looks out at the audience.)* I never can remember how to spell that word. Lonely. Without an "e"? Or with an "e." Hmmm, with, I think.

(He exits, just as WOMAN enters, wearing a trench coat. She sits at the table.)

WOMAN: To ... whom ... it ... may ... concern. My friends inform me that I do not have a complaining nature. The earth ... and the fullness thereof ... is perfectly evident to me, and if that earth were to be divided between the privileged and the underprivileged, I would count myself among the ... the former. Nevertheless, I am ... *(Long pause.)* I don't know why ... but I am ... terribly ... unbearably ... lonely.

(She glides away, just as MICHAEL and SALLY enter.)

MICHAEL: Thanks ... a lot ... for all the good stuff I've got. Like ...

SALLY: Having a house, lots of ...

MICHAEL: Food, clothes ...

SALLY *and* MICHAEL: TV.

MICHAEL: I sure do have a lot of ...

SALLY and MICHAEL: Fun.

MICHAEL: But sometimes ...

SALLY: Sometimes I just wish I ...

MICHAEL: I just wish I was, you know ...

SALLY: Not so lonely.

MICHAEL: Lonesome.

SALLY: Alone.

> *(MICHAEL and SALLY exit, as MAN ONE and WOMAN enter talking. They are dressed identically, and each carries a briefcase. MAN ONE has a notebook computer. From this point, the scene moves very quickly.)*

WOMAN: *(With a sheaf of papers in her hand.)* We're being swamped! *(Holding up the letters in her hand.)* Look. More. Every day it's the same thing. And always the same complaint.

MAN ONE: *(Sitting down at the table.)* All this lonely-baloney stuff. Could be a fad.

WOMAN: Or a trick.

MAN ONE: Next year it'll be something else they want.

WOMAN: I don't know, these files go waaay back, all the way back to—*(Searches in briefcase.)*

MAN ONE: I'd put it down to unrealistic expectations. Every man is an island onto himself—and every woman and child too, of course. That was settled long ago.

WOMAN: That's the way it is, I agree, but maybe—

MAN ONE: I don't know. Our mandate is for—

WOMAN: Market research! A parliamentary inquiry!

MAN ONE: A parliamentary inquiry? On human loneliness? We'd be laughed out of office.

WOMAN: I could go with a feasibility study. Could be a good move. Politically.

MAN ONE: We could start with—

WOMAN: With us.

MAN ONE: With us?

WOMAN: Haven't you ever ... in the middle of the night ... or even in the middle of the day ... Haven't you ever wished ... I mean, all this island stuff! Get real! What I'm saying is ... what if there's another way to ... like sometimes I ache, I just ache to ... lean ... on someone ... else.

MAN ONE: Lean? On someone? Else?

WOMAN: Haven't you ever ... wanted to be a part of something larger?

MAN ONE: A club, you mean? A professional association? I already belong—

WOMAN: I'm talking about, you know, belonging to some*one.*

MAN ONE: Slavery was outlawed back in—

WOMAN: Some*one* belonging to you kind-of-thing. You know?

(MAN TWO enters wearing a black derby hat and carrying a pile of papers, a thermos of coffee, and a stack of paper cups. He pours coffee into the cups.)

MAN TWO: Excuse me. I think I know what you mean.

WOMAN: *(Checking her watch.)* We've been waiting for you. I thought this meeting was called for three o'clock.

MAN TWO: Sorry. I've been going through all this correspondence. *(Sets a pile of papers on table.)* Hundreds of letters, faxes, memos. It's appalling. Something has to be done.

WOMAN: Exactly what I've been saying. But apparently it's unconstitutional to—

MAN TWO: Units. The solution is units! That's what I've come up with. That's my concept.

MAN ONE: *(Whipping out a clipboard.)* Units?

MAN TWO: Social units. I've correlated the complaints and petitions, put them into categories A, B, and C, and extracted the common elements and drawn a curve of ascending desperation which intersects with the line of basic human need and extrapolated down to a solution which—look, it's all here on the fact sheet.

WOMAN: *(Excited.)* And your conclusion is—

MAN TWO: Small social units. Or cells if you like.

MAN ONE: Unworkable.

MAN TWO: We could start with units of two. One male, one female? What d'ya think?

WOMAN: That makes sense biologically but—

MAN ONE: But will it stand up in the courts?

WOMAN: Is it enforceable?

MAN TWO: We'll keep it optional, but once the social and economic model demonstrates its viability—

MAN ONE: I suppose it could catch on. If—

MAN TWO: One male, one female per unit, but with legislation allowing for *(Holds up finger, for emphasis.)* group ... growth.

WOMAN: God, I love it.

MAN ONE: The symmetry! It's almost, well, sort of *nuclear.* But can we sell it.

MAN TWO: I thought we'd call it—Is someone taking notes here?

MAN ONE: *(Typing furiously on computer.)* I'm inputting as fast as I can.

MAN TWO: I thought we'd blend the two elements of each unit, male and female, and call it a female-male-ie.

MAN ONE: *(Writing.)* Or, to compress just a bit, fee-mal-ie. Catchy.

MAN TWO: Ahem. Actually, my thought was that we'd put the accent on the first syllable. Fee-mal-ie.

WOMAN: Or how about contracting that into "family"?

MAN ONE: Brilliant. Fami-*ly* singular, famil-*ies* plural. Let's go with it.

ALL: Families.

> *(The lights dim as the word "families" echoes. Light and music crescendo to suggest time passing; lights come up on the three actors standing at attention reading long computer print-outs.)*

WOMAN: *(Reading.)* ... And each unit permitted two members—or whatever grouping legislation defines—

MAN TWO: ... to share common domicile and pursue common ends which—

MAN ONE: ... which will be mutually beneficial to each unit—

WOMAN: ... and beneficial to succeeding unit components who will be added from time to time. *(Lowers her paper.)* Well, I'll say this, it's imaginative.

> *(She folds up the paper and exits while the two men sit at the table. One pulls out a bottle and two brandy snifters and pours; they stand as if at a club. Light and music crescendo, quicker this time, to suggest time passing.)*

MAN ONE: The whole thing is contrary to human dynamics. That's my belief.

MAN TWO: Remember, it's strictly optional. And it solves more than the loneliness quotient. Think of the economic value.

MAN ONE: You guarantee it'll be kept flexible? Things have a way of getting ... entrenched. They go out of fashion and then—

MAN TWO: The last thing we want are rigid patterns in our families—

MAN ONE: Families, shamilies. Read my lips, it'll never catch the public imagination.

> *(Time passing crescendo again, faster still. They change position. WOMAN re-enters and stands at stage left.)*

WOMAN: *(Looking up.)* But is it progressive or regressive? That's what I'd like to know.

> *(They sit at the table, and face the audience as if conducting a press conference.)*

MAN ONE: Ladies and gentlemen, we have had the pleasure this evening of learning more about the proposed fam-i-ly *(Stumbles, as though pronouncing a foreign word.)* system and some of the ramifications of—

MAN TWO: Of course—just let me reiterate what I said earlier—there are a few wrinkles to be ironed out before the plan is officially inaugurated.

VOICE OVER: I would like to address a question to the chair.

MAN ONE: This is an open forum.

VOICE OVER: My concern is with, well, what about duplication of labour?

MAN TWO: *(Rising, assuming the stance of listener.)* My concern exactly, exactly. I've already written to the editor, the editor, about this very question, this very question. Duplication of labour.

VOICE OVER: How precisely does the government intend to resolve this issue?

MAN TWO: How precisely does the government intend to resolve this issue?

MAN ONE: This whole thing seems like a tempest in a tea—

WOMAN: I wish I could believe that.

MAN ONE: Surely duplication of labour can be sorted out in each individual unit.

WOMAN: Perhaps, but let's not leave it to—

MAN TWO: I agree with you both, I absolutely agree. But I still feel we need some kind of structure within which we can establish guidelines.

WOMAN: As long as they're only guidelines—

MAN TWO: All right then, are you ready?

MAN ONE: Ready.

WOMAN: Ready.

> *(MAN TWO places his hat on the table.)*

MAN TWO: The rules have been explained. You *(To WOMAN.)* will draw on the side of female labour, and you *(To MAN ONE.)* for the male component.

MAN ONE: *(Reaching into the hat, his eyes shut. He pulls out a paper and reads.)* Hunting. *(Smiles.)* Hunting!

MAN TWO: *(Writing this down.)* Males, hunting. *(Nods at WOMAN.)* Your turn.

WOMAN: *(Drawing out a paper and reading.)* Gathering? What's that supposed to—What exactly am I supposed to gather?

MAN TWO: Ready for round two?

MAN ONE: *(Drawing again and reading.)* Protection of unit. Does that mean full responsibility? That seems rather—

MAN TWO: *(Writing busily.)* Male. Protection of unit.

WOMAN: *(Drawing again and reading.)* Child-bearing. Hey, wait a minute—

MAN TWO: Let's move right along here.

MAN ONE: Provisioning and maintenance of shelter. Navigation of the high seas. I can't even swim—

WOMAN: Child-rearing?

(MAN ONE draws another paper, reads, crumples it, and puts it back.)

MAN TWO: *(Retrieves the paper and reads it out loud.)* Swineherding, sheep shearing, animal husbandry.

WOMAN: *(Carefully stirring the papers before extracting one.)* Cleaning. Sweeping. Scrubbing! *(She puts her head on the table.)*

MAN ONE: Exploration. Discovery.

WOMAN: Hospitality. Tending fires.

MAN ONE : Jurisprudence. Execution.

WOMAN: Care of the sick. Mourning the dead.

MAN ONE: Invention.

WOMAN: Application.

MAN ONE: Mores.

WOMAN: Manners.

MAN ONE: Expansion of territories.

WOMAN: Spinning, weaving. Now wait just a minute—

MAN ONE: Investing of wealth.

WOMAN: Consumer activities.

MAN ONE: Creation of ritual.

WOMAN: Perpetration of ritual.

MAN ONE: Education, politics.

WOMAN: Morality. And—I do not believe this—peace!

MAN TWO: *(Shakes the bowl upside down; only one piece of paper falls out. He reads it.)* All other duties to be shared and negotiated. And now—are you ready?

(He pulls two paper doll-style wedding costumes from the briefcase, and puts them on the other two. MAN ONE and WOMAN rise; there is a burst of wedding music. They join their hands over the table.)

MAN ONE: Till death us do part.

(They exit arm-in-arm, in time to the music.)

MAN TWO: *(Speaking to the audience.)* We believe that the new family system is strengthened by a public act of commitment, a tangible example that the public can grasp and pattern itself on and—

> (*MICHAEL runs on to stage, wearing a sort of messenger's cap. He hands MAN TWO a sealed envelope and exits while MAN TWO slowly, with the aid of a letter opener, opens the seal.*)

MAN TWO: (*Reading.*) Amendment to Family Act. In case of incompatibility ... (*He stops and looks up questioningly.*) Incompatibility? Hey, we never thought of incompatibility ... It seems something has been overlooked here.

WOMAN TWO: (*Rushing in with her briefcase, extracting a letter from it.*) Amendment Two to Family Act. In case of gay couples— Gay couples?

MAN ONE: We forgot completely about gay couples. And— (*Reading.*) good heavens, listen to this: it appears some people are holding out. Thousands of them, in fact. A significant demographic sector. They claim, they actually claim, they prefer to live alone, in units of one!

MAN TWO: Let me make a note of that.

MAN ONE: You know what I think? This whole family thing is going to blow our credibility.

MAN TWO: We've got to shelve this idea and I mean quick.

WOMAN TWO: I knew there'd be a snag. Didn't I tell you—

MAN ONE: Back to the drawing board.

MAN TWO: (*Wistful.*) And it had such possibilities.

WOMAN TWO: Yes, well, workability's the bottom line and families just—

MAN ONE: (*Grabbing papers.*) It's into the shredder, I'm afraid.

MAN TWO: Couldn't we just—

WOMAN TWO: If only—

MAN ONE: (*Overlapping.*) If only—

MAN TWO: (*Overlapping.*) If only—

WOMAN TWO: Wait. I've got a brilliant idea. Let's set up a model. A trial unit—the prototype nuclear family, male, female, two appendages—and see how it works. One model won't do. We'd need a hundred families.

MAN ONE: A thousand! And we'd need time for it to develop.

WOMAN TWO: Decades. Generations. A long, long, time. What I suggest is ...

> *(The sound of canned applause, and the stirring of marching music on piano as the actors exit chatting to each other.)*

Scene Two

> *(Lights dim slightly and a screen is lowered showing a blueprint of the house. A REAL ESTATE AGENT enters, jingling keys. He speaks quickly; there are no pregnant pauses. He uses real estate patter, but with true sincerity.)*

REAL ESTATE AGENT: ... An excellent property. Quiet neighbourhood, gracious tree-lined street, solid foundation, roof, chimney, flashing, and here—*(Pauses while the screen is removed and goes to switch on the light over the door.)*—you have your outdoor light. Which some call a burglar light. And others, of a different disposition and outlook, *(Snaps light on and off.)* refer to as a welcome light. Now in my professional opinion this house should suit our trial-balloon family of four. Family-of-four. *(Relishing the words.)* Most of our new government projections, you know, are made for that fantasy in the sky *(Rolls his eyes.)* family-of-four. Your mother and father, your son and daughter. Your patriarchal set-up. Mother and father both employed, for the moment, but keeping their fingers crossed about the future. Health reasonable. Debts manageable. Family members morally accountable. What we are seeing here is a fairly accurate, but improbable and randomly unaccountable statistical model.

> *(He steps into kitchen which becomes suddenly lit. MOTHER is frozen in front of stove, oven door half open. The AGENT ignores her.)*

The kitchen, ladies and gentlemen, la cuisine. Centre-piece of this model domicile, heart of the residence. Recently updated. Notice hooks for family outerwear. His, hers, his, hers, didn't I tell you?—family-of-four! And let's see—we have *(Ticking off the items.)* practical work surfaces, cupboards, dishwasher, microwave and fridge. *(Opens fridge which gives off a blue sci-fi light and a deep sigh is heard; the sound ceases when he closes the door.)* The heart of the heart of the family. *(Turns to the audience.)* An important piece of family mythology has it that all serious issues are raised and resolved in the food preparation area. We don't yet know what these family issues will be, of course—we can only speculate.

(He walks into the living room; lights go off in the kitchen area and come on in the living room. FATHER is frozen into position, seated on an ottoman, hunched over his newspaper.)

A living room, the fulcrum of the house, the anchor of the home. Where our putative family of four finds ease and a sense of their own microcosmic community. It's here that family ceremonies are performed, though we don't yet know what these ceremonies will consist of. A living room—please notice particularly the oak trim, you don't find that anymore—is widely acknowledged to be that anointed space where the model family *(Pause.)* connects. *(Pause.)* Or doesn't connect. We're not sure how this connection business will—well, it looks good on paper, I'll say that.

(Lights go out, and then come up as strong sunlight through Sally's upstairs bedroom.)

Scene Three

(SALLY, dressed in jeans, is frozen, leaning in front of a mirror, examining her skin.)

SALLY: Now, here before you is a fairly typical child's or teenager's bedroom. Bed *(Pats the bed.)* room. A refuge. A place of privacy for individual family members and yet! Yet never far from the resonating pulse of the family unit. Within these protective walls many a family crisis is aired or *(Pause.)* not aired—Notice how bright this room is? Marvellous French window. Southern exposure. Lets in light but—*(Consults her clipboard.)* It seems it has been sealed shut by owner. *(Tests the window.)* Not to be opened, it says here. Not ever.

(The light through the window snaps off and comes up on Michael's room. MICHAEL is frozen into a headstand position.)

Here we have the second child's room. Child, according to legislation, means anything from one week to twelve or eighteen years, the term is flexible. We are all, in a sense, children, the inhabitants of children's rooms. Here we can hide. Here we can perform strange acts and rituals. You can almost sense the unrevealed mysteries of human lives in such rumpled corners, can't you? And yet, there are palpable certainties too—the bed, the curtains, the

Errata

The corrected pages 18 and 19 of this errata
replace pages 18 and 19 of the bound publication.

and resolved in the food preparation area. We don't yet know what these family issues will be, of course—we can only speculate.

(He walks into the living room; lights go off in the kitchen area and come on in the living room. FATHER is frozen into position, seated on an ottoman, hunched over his newspaper.)

A living room, the fulcrum of the house, the anchor of the home. Where our putative family of four finds ease and a sense of their own microcosmic community. It's here that family ceremonies are performed, though we don't yet know what these ceremonies will consist of. A living room—please notice particularly the oak trim, you don't find that anymore—is widely acknowledged to be that anointed space where the model family *(Pause.)* connects. *(Pause.)* Or doesn't connect. We're not sure how this connection business will—well, it looks good on paper, I'll say that.

(Lights go down on the living room, and then come up as strong sunlight through Sally's upstairs bedroom. SALLY, dressed in jeans, is frozen, leaning in front of a mirror, examining her skin.)

Now, here before you is a fairly typical child's or teenager's bedroom. Bed *(Pats the bed.)* room. A refuge. A place of privacy for individual family members and yet! Yet never far from the resonating pulse of the family unit. Within these protective walls many a family crisis is aired or *(Pause.)* not aired—Notice how bright this room is? Marvellous French window. Southern exposure. Lets in light but—*(Consults her clipboard.)* It seems it has been sealed shut by owner. *(Tests the window.)* Not to be opened, it says here. Not ever.

(The light through the window snaps off and comes up on Michael's room. MICHAEL is frozen into a headstand position.)

Here we have the second child's room. Child, according to legislation, means anything from one week to twelve or eighteen years, the term is flexible. We are all, in a sense, children, the inhabitants of children's rooms. Here, we can hide. Here we can perform strange acts and rituals. You can almost sense the unrevealed mysteries of human lives in such rumpled corners, can't you? And yet, there are palpable certainties too—the bed, the curtains, the sense of confinement which will sometimes swallow up our family members, but offer ... a blessed asylum. The committee has thought of everything. And so, here it is. *(With a flourish.)* The House!

(Lights go on one by one all over the house, all darken for a second, then come up brightly so that all the rooms are revealed.)

A visible and, in my opinion, a highly charged metaphor for the family as we idealize it.

Scene Three

(Music begins to play.)

FATHER: *(From the living room, putting down the paper, he stands and addresses the audience.)* Metaphor? The word family means people in a house together, look it up in a dictionary. And a house is something definable, specific. If you lived somewhere else you'd be someone else. A house, an apartment, a dwelling, a shelter of some kind—Why, it's much, much more than a metaphor. What I mean is, real estate is real, not a flimsy stage setting. It's—

MOTHER: *(From the kitchen.)* A roof is a roof is a roof. As the saying goes.

FATHER: Think about it. *(Singing.)*
We commence,
All of us, with a place of res-i-dence.

MOTHER: I absolutely agree. *(Singing.)*
A family must give,
Thought to where they live.

(The song takes on a rockabilly rhythm.)

ALL:
Walls and floors, ceilings and doors,
A window to let in air.
A family needs a base, a place,
A family needs a so-o-o-mewhere,
A house is more.

FATHER:
A family must give consideration,
To a place of habitation.

ALL:
A base, a place,
A so-o-o-mewhere.
A house is more.

Scene 4 (a)

*(Music. This scene is played very quickly, like a speeded-up
movie, and is announced by an overhead electric title or by an
actor carrying a sign across the stage that says "A Typical
Day." There is the sound of ticking clocks, and then the sound
of alarm clocks going off, and clock radios turning on upstairs.
Simultaneously MOTHER watches TV while FATHER moves to
the kitchen, banging pans, singing loudly. Four different sound
systems fight against each other while each family member
prepares for the day: SALLY and MICHAEL putting on sweat-
ers, brushing their hair; FATHER setting cereal bowls on the
table; MOTHER staring continually at the TV screen until she
rises, runs to kitchen, and rings the dinner gong. The noise from
the sound systems stop at the same instant all over the house.
They all mime peering into a nearby mirror for a minute,
examining and preparing their faces, and then rush to kitchen
table.)*

FATHER: I have so terribly much to do today, so many concerns. I
hardly know where to begin. There's an appointment at nine sharp
and already I'm running late—

MOTHER: *(Simultaneously with FATHER's speech.)* I should have
looked over my notes. Am I going to be late for my meeting? Am
I going to get the car started? I'm running late—

SALLY: My hair, it looks like hell, my face has broken out again, I
like this sweater though, it makes me look just like Isabella Rosellini
in that picture of—

MICHAEL: *(Spoken simultaneously with SALLY's speech.)* Math
test, math test, my head hurts, I hate morning, I love Shredded
Wheat, math test, fifty per cent at least, she's taken all the milk,
what's the point of—

*(They all abruptly fall silent, eat away with their spoons, then
start speaking in overlapping speeches again.)*

FATHER: Do they appreciate all they have?

MOTHER: *(Overlapping.)* Does anyone ever say thank you?

SALLY: Doesn't anyone ever look at me, really look at me?

MICHAEL: *(Overlapping with SALLY.)* Does anyone say, good luck on your stupid math test.

> *(They fall silent again, while the clock ticks and a microwave dings. Everyone rises in one synchronized motion, grabs books, bags, and coats from hooks. Each pauses an instant to look in a mirror, pat their hair in a synchronized motion, and then leave. A clock ticks quickly; the lights darken outside; lamps go on inside. A door opens, and the family rushes in one by one, hangs coats on hooks; Michael's coat immediately falls off the hook.)*

FATHER: What a day, not a minute to myself, just hope there's time to read the paper tonight.

MOTHER: *(Simultaneously.)* Too much salt, not enough sugar, over-cooked, forgot to pick up milk, all that work I brought home—

SALLY: I got three compliments on my sweater, one was from a boy, I can't eat that, I'm allergic to that.

MICHAEL: *(Simultaneously.)* Hey, it was a breeze, I whizzed through, almost got the last problem finished even—

> *(They fall silent. Sound of ticking clock. FATHER rushes to the living room to put on the TV, MOTHER clears plates from the table, and the children go upstairs and lie on their beds. Lights go down all over house while the sound of the ticking clock resounds and there is one final microwave ding. A long sorrowful sound of dog barking is heard in the distance until complete silence. The sign, either shown on the screen overhead or carried by an actor, says: "End of a Typical Day.")*

sense of confinement which will sometimes swallow up our family members, but offer ... a blessed asylum. The committee has thought of everything. And so, here it is. *(With a flourish.)* The House!

(Lights go on one by one all over the house, all darken for a second, then come up brightly so that all the rooms are revealed.)

A visible and, in my opinion, a highly charged metaphor for the family as we idealize it.

(Music begins to play.)

FATHER: *(From the living room, putting down the paper, he stands and addresses the audience.)* Metaphor? The word family means people in a house together, look it up in a dictionary. And a house is something definable, specific. If you lived somewhere else you'd be someone else. A house, an apartment, a dwelling, a shelter of some kind—Why, it's much, much more than a metaphor. What I mean is, real estate is real, not a flimsy stage setting. It's—

MOTHER: *(From the kitchen.)* A roof is a roof is a roof. As the saying goes.

FATHER: Think about it. *(Singing.)*
We commence,
All of us, with a place of res-i-dence.

MOTHER: I absolutely agree. *(Singing.)*
A family must give,
Thought to where they live.

(The song takes on a rockabilly rhythm.)

ALL:
Walls and floors, ceilings and doors,
A window to let in air.
A family needs a base, a place,
A family needs a so-o-o-mewhere,
A house is more.

FATHER:
A family must give consideration,
To a place of habitation.

ALL:
A base, a place,
A so-o-o-mewhere.
A house is more.

MICHAEL: *(Speaking.)* Hey, no one likes to get tied down, that's
for sure, but I guess in the final analysis a family needs ...

SALLY: *(Speaking.)* ... an address.

ALL: *(Singing.)*
Somewhere to live, somewhere to be,
Somewhere to be—
A fam-i-ly.

MOTHER: *(Speaking.)* You know, the way I think of it ... a family
unit doesn't make a whole lot of sense without a—

MICHAEL: *(Speaking.)* —a picket fence?

SALLY: Forget your picket fence, this is 1995. *(Half speaking,
half singing.)* If the family unit is going to survive ...

ALL: *(Singing.)*
It needs definition,
It needs absolute space ...

MICHAEL: *(Speaking.)* A fireplace?

FATHER: *(Speaking.)* Strictly optional, I'd say no. Now a furnace is
more to the point, or one of these *(Singing.)* new solar-powered
heat exchangers—

ALL: *(Singing.)*
Walls and floors, ceilings and doors,
A window to let in air.
A family needs a base, a place,
A family needs a so-o-o-mewhere.

MICHAEL: *(Speaking.)* There are homeless people, you know. Let's
not forget—

SALLY: *(Speaking.)* About that window, I hate to keep coming down
on this topic, this issue, but wouldn't it be nice, I mean wouldn't
it be sort of, you know, a good idea, Mom? Dad? If we could ...
really, you know, like open this window now and then?

MOTHER: Shhhhhh. That's enough.

FATHER: Not up for discussion.

MOTHER: We never open that window.

FATHER: Never.

> *(They all fall silent for a beat or two, and then start to sing
> again.)*

ALL:

A house is more,
Than a metaphor.
A house encloses, comforts, keeps you warm,
From virtual reality storms.

Solid walls, and substantial floors,
Water pipes, slamming doors.
A house is more, more than a metaphor.

A shelf, a lamp, an easy chair,
A curtain pulled against the air,
A house is more
A family needs a so-o-o-mewhere.
A house is more ...

> *(MICHAEL and SALLY move to lie on their beds, while MOTHER and FATHER settle together on the sofa.)*

A bed, a place to put your head
A place, a base,
A so-o-o-mewhere.
A house is more.

> *(The house darkens.)*

Scene Four

(Morning light comes up slowly on Michael's bedroom.)

MICHAEL: *(Standing, he puts on a baseball cap, and speaks to the audience.)* Hello there. I'm the son. You can call me, uhhhh, Michael.

MOTHER: *(Calling.)* Michael.

FATHER: *(Calling sharply.)* Michael!

SALLY: *(Exasperated.)* Michael.

MICHAEL: Okay, so I'm Michael, the youngest in the family, the only boy. Am I spoiled? Yeah, maybe a little.

MOTHER, FATHER, *and* SALLY: *(Overlapping.)* A little!

MICHAEL: I'm the adventurous type—but the kind that doesn't do or say anything yet. I'm moody, like that guy ...

SALLY: James Dean.

MICHAEL: What more can I tell you? Interests? Well, once I made one of those model airplanes. Another time I started a rock collection, but that only lasted one day.

MOTHER *and* FATHER: *(Overlapping.)* One afternoon.

MICHAEL: The fact is, I've still got a nightlight in my room.

SALLY: Yeah, Mickey Mouse.

MICHAEL: I'm not quite a person yet. I'm still getting, you know, ready.

> *(Lights fade and come back up in Sally's room.)*

SALLY: Hi. I'm the daughter. Self-centered teenager sulking in her teenage-y room. Which is ... I mean, look at it ... a ...

MOTHER: A disgusting mess.

SALLY: But a mess that is more or less tolerated, for the moment, anyway, that's how the family—

MOTHER, FATHER, *and* MICHAEL: *(Together.)* Is handling it!

SALLY: My name is *(Pause.)* Sally?

MICHAEL: Sally!

MOTHER: Sally?

FATHER: *(Calling.)* Sal-ly!

SALLY: Yeah, Sally. I don't like to talk about myself all that much, never, in fact, but if someone came out and asked me to describe myself I'd say that there are, well, hundreds and hundreds of deep, deep, layers to my personality. Good layers and we-ei-rd layers.

MOTHER: Uh-huh.

SALLY: And one thing more you should know about me. I cry ... at least once every day.

> *(The lights fade in Sally's bedroom and come up in the kitchen, where FATHER is opening the fridge door, poking his finger into it, and then licking his finger.)*

FATHER: Good evening, I'm the father. And husband. I earn money and try to be humane and agreeable and not— *(He spies a neighbour out the window and calls out.)* Clark! I'll bring the drill bits over this afternoon. *(Returns his attention back to audience.)* — and not come on, you know, too heavy, too ...

MOTHER: Patriarchal.

FATHER: Like I've got power in our unit, but we all pretend I don't. I also have a real name, Brian.

MOTHER: *(Calling.)* Brian.

MICHAEL *and* SALLY: *(Slightly mocking.)* Brian.

FATHER: But it's strictly arbitrary. How did I become a husband and father? It was just something that happened to me, and I ... I welcomed it. It struck me across the eyes one day, the person I could be, husband, father, and ever since I've been walking around, sort of ... sort of blinking.

> *(The lights fade in the kitchen and go up in living room, where MOTHER is turning off the TV.)*

MOTHER: I'm the mother. Called ...

SALLY: Mum.

MICHAEL: Mummy.

FATHER: Honey, sweetheart.

MOTHER: Et cetera, et cetera. My real name is Jane.

SALLY: Brian's wife.

MOTHER: Slightly out-of-shape mother of two fairly typical offspring. Sally and Michael, their names are. I try to keep things functioning around here. And I try very, very hard to keep things light. That's spelled L-I-T-E. A tough job but I've learned to do it. I've learned to keep my sorrow dark and secret, to keep it from ... spreading. Sorrow can find its way into every room ... every corner, if you let it. I hum under my breath quite a lot and whistle little tunes ...

> *(MICHAEL whistles under her words.)*

and make cooing sounds, and say "uh huh" when someone tells me something really, really awful.

SALLY: Uh huh.

MOTHER: That kind of thing. Now, what I thought I would do is take you through an average day in this household, okay? *(Lights go off.)*

Scene Five

> *(The sound of birds chirping. Lights come up on Michael's bedroom, where he is standing on his head. MOTHER enters.)*

MOTHER: Oh, there you are, Michael. Well! Happy birthday, love.

> *(MICHAEL grunts.)*

My Michael's growing up. Before you know it you'll—

MICHAEL: Uh huh.

MOTHER: Now Michael, I have a question. I need your cooperation. I've been looking all over this house for your jean jacket.

MICHAEL: *(Remaining on his head.)* It's under the bed.

MOTHER: Where?

MICHAEL: Under the bed. I think. *(Stands upright.)*

MOTHER: Good. *(Crooning.)* Now Michael, listen to me, the time has come. I hope you don't mind but I'm going to wash your jacket today. *(Angrily.)* And I'm going to—*(Sweetly.)* Are you listening? *(Angrily.)* I'm going to iron it too.

MICHAEL: I like it dirty. I like it wrinkled. But thanks for the offer.

MOTHER: You can't go to Grandma and Grandpa's tonight with a dirty jacket. I mean, I don't personally care about that kind of thing. As a bona fide survivor of the sixties I'm not uptight in that way, I respect difference and allow for variant behaviours. It's a fact that grooming and cleanliness are more relaxed these days than they ever were *(Suddenly loud and angry.)* in your grandmother's day, but *(Softening.)* when people get older they tend to make judgments—

MICHAEL: No.

MOTHER: *(Confidingly.)* Michael, I want to tell you something about *(Angrily.)* your grandmother. *(Softly.)* Are you listening? When your grandmother was a young girl, eighteen, nineteen, from a very poor family, incredibly poor, you would not believe how poor that family was, well, she got a scholarship to go to teachers' training college, and can you guess how many dresses she had to her name?

MICHAEL: *(Guessing.)* One?

MOTHER: Two. Just two dresses. Her whole wardrobe. Imagine. Every night she'd wash one of her dresses and that night she'd have to get the other one all neat and ironed and mended for the next day. Looking fresh and attractive was extremely important to her. And to her parents before her. To present a neat appearance. That meant something. Appearance is more than, you know, just appearances. It says a whole lot about the inner you. And about the home you come from. The values of that home. What they represent. That's how she felt. She did that for two years. Now what I'm saying—

MICHAEL: No, Mom.

MOTHER: *(Angrily shouting.)* I'm saying that my mother, your grandmother, has this unholy relentless fixation on what people are going to think. *(Sweetly, speaking softly.)* She does not see the point of grime and grunge, Michael. She would never understand in a million years how a person could *(Suddenly angry again.)* take a pair of scissors and actually cut holes in a perfectly good jean jacket—

MICHAEL: It just wore like that—

MOTHER: Uh huh. Anyway, all I want is to make your jacket a little more presentable *(Suddenly angry.)* for Grandma, *(Softening.)* a little soap and water, and I'll cut off some of those loose threads around the sleeves—

MICHAEL: *(Pleading.)* Just one more week. I'll put it in the wash next week.

MOTHER: Is that a promise?

MICHAEL: Maybe.

MOTHER: Sorry, what was that you said?

> *(MICHAEL grunts. MOTHER leaves. FATHER enters.)*

FATHER: Oh, there you are. Just wanted a word or two with you, son.

MICHAEL: *(Still standing on his head.)* Yeah?

FATHER: Happy birthday.

MICHAEL: Thanks. *(He stands upright.)*

FATHER: You know, son, I've never been one to put all that much importance on physical appearances, that is, on exterior considerations—

MICHAEL: Here we go …

FATHER: Michael, look, you know I don't care about superficial—

MICHAEL: Uh huh, I know. *(Returns to headstand position.)*

FATHER: But that … jacket you've been wearing lately. It's just a little on the … scruffy side, know what I mean?

MICHAEL: I like it.

FATHER: You wouldn't want people to think—I mean, we're going to Grandma and Grandpa's for dinner tonight, Grandma's probably made you a special cake, one of her three-layer *(Angry.)* nightmares, *(Softening.)* and she might look at you and think—

MICHAEL: I like it, I like it, I really do like it.

FATHER: It's Saturday, son, the whole day's free. Hey, how about we go down to the mall this morning, the two of us—it's your birthday after all—and see if we could find something a bit more—

MICHAEL: Next year, okay? *(Stands upright again.)* Next time around.

FATHER: But don't you care if *(Angry.)* Grandma—

MICHAEL: No. No, no, no. I care, but I don't care ... enough.

FATHER: Mind if I tell you a story.

MICHAEL: Go ahead.

FATHER: Well, when I was a boy, hmmmm, there was another boy in our class and he had very, very strict parents. Every day after school—well, can you just guess what they made him do every day after school?

MICHAEL: *(Pause.)* No.

FATHER: They made that young boy, twelve, thirteen years of age, go straight home and polish his shoes.

MICHAEL: Every day, huh.

FATHER: Amazing, isn't it. These days we'd call it abuse. The rest of us would be playing baseball or larking around or goofing off or whatever, and this kid would be on his way home to polish his shoes. Well, I guess we thought that was pretty terrible at the time, having to do that every single day, but do you know what?

MICHAEL: What?

FATHER: Today, that little boy is president of United Insurance Corporation of Canada. And chairman of the board of Trade. There isn't a person on Bay Street who doesn't know and respect his name. His picture very often appears in the business pages of *The Globe and Mail!* And so, Michael, I think you can understand now what I'm saying.

MICHAEL: *(After a long pause.)* Well ... you didn't shine your shoes every day and you've done okay. Haven't you?

FATHER: But compared to—?

MICHAEL: Yeah, what?

FATHER: This person I'm telling you about ...

MICHAEL: This big shot insurance guy?

FATHER: He didn't get where he got because of destiny. He got there because of rigorous training, because of character development. He couldn't miss. He became the person he was. This motivated, focused human being. That's what we do—we are what we were. Remember that, son. We are what we were. That's how I—

MICHAEL: Why are you trying to scare me?

FATHER: I'm just saying that it's here, it's now, that things happen. It's in your home, your family, these formative years, that you find your, your ...

MICHAEL: *(Speaks desperately.)* My what?

FATHER: *(Faltering.)* Your identity, sort of. Who you are.

MICHAEL: Now you're really scaring me.

FATHER: So, well, maybe now you see what I'm talking about. About this jacket of yours—

MICHAEL: Wait a minute, wait a minute. You just about had me for a minute there, all that stuff about the guy shining his shoes, you just about had a hammerlock on my brain, you got me all twisted up, but no. No. I do ... not ... want ... a new jacket.

FATHER: *(Exits, shaking his head and muttering.)* I was only trying. This man's picture, I mean, he's in *(In an awed tone.)* The Globe and Mail, frequently. Think about it, son, you could—

(MICHAEL resumes standing on his head. SALLY enters.)

SALLY: Hey, Michael, I've got a favour to ask you.

MICHAEL: *(Still on his head.)* Yuh?

SALLY: You know your jean jacket?

MICHAEL: Yuh.

SALLY: Can I borrow it?

MICHAEL: I thought you hated my jean jacket. You said I looked like a scuzz.

SALLY: I just said that.

MICHAEL: *(Pause.)* Why?

SALLY: I don't know. I was ... jealous. I mean, that jacket of yours is a really neat piece of clothing. It makes you look ... revolutionary and ... attractive.

MICHAEL: *(Pause.)* You don't think Grandma's going to—?

SALLY: Look, I really need to borrow it today. Your jacket. For something special.

MICHAEL: Like what?

SALLY: A secret, sort of. But, don't worry, it's a good secret.

MICHAEL: Good for who?

SALLY: You'll see.

MICHAEL: You better not get it ripped off.

SALLY: *(Scooping up the jacket and exiting.)* I'll take good care of it, trust me.

　　(The lights dim.)

Scene Six

　　(Lights come up on the family in the living room. MOTHER, FATHER and SALLY are singing.)

MOTHER, FATHER, SALLY:
Happy birthday dear Michael,
Happy birthday to you.

SALLY: *(Handing MICHAEL a box.)* Open mine first.

　　(MICHAEL tears open the box and pulls out his jean jacket which has been embroidered all over and trimmed with gold braid.)

MICHAEL: Is this my—?

SALLY: I worked all day on it. Hours and hours. Kelly helped me. And Patty and Tracy. And Laurie and Tiffany.

MICHAEL: My jean jacket! You took it and you—

SALLY: We got the idea from this article we read in the paper, the leisure section. Everyone in New York is starting to wear retro jackets just like this. And even Toronto. Here, try it on.

MICHAEL: *(Slips it on slowly.)* I wouldn't be seen dead—

MOTHER: At least the dirt won't show as much.

SALLY: This gold ribbon stuff on the shoulders? That was Tiffany's idea.

MICHAEL: *(Looking interested.)* Tiffany? Really?

FATHER: We're going to be late for Grandma's—

SALLY: Well, birthday brother, didn't I say I had a great surprise for you!

MICHAEL: I trusted you.

MOTHER: *(In a singsong voice.)* I think you're forgetting something, Michael.

MICHAEL: What?

FATHER: Don't you have something to say to your sister, Michael?

MICHAEL: *(Turns and regards himself in the mirror.)* Thanks. *(Turns again, pleased with his image, posing.)* Thanks ... a lot.

> *(He wears the jacket for the rest of the play. Happy birthday music fades out as the lights go down.)*

Scene Seven

> *(The lights come up on the lower level of the house. MOTHER is staring into a blank TV screen, MICHAEL is sprawled on the floor, SALLY is doing homework at the kitchen table, and FATHER is standing at the open fridge door, snacking. The doorbell rings. SALLY gets up to answer and opens the door to the FRET-and-WORRY MANAGEMENT CONSULTANT, an androgynous character who resembles a Clinique consultant, efficient, wearing a smock and carrying a bag; the character's goodness shines through.)*

SALLY: Oh, it's you. Oh! I didn't know—I mean, we forgot you were coming today.

CONSULTANT: It's the third Thursday of the month. Our scheduled date.

FATHER: *(Calling out to SALLY.)* Who is it, Sally?

SALLY: It's the Fret-and-Worry consultant.

FATHER: Oh, of course, of course, come right in, let me take your coat.

CONSULTANT: It is our regular day. But please don't become worried, and certainly not fretful, about forgetting our appointment. It is important, however, that we document on-going stresses so that we can work together on ...

FATHER: Oh, yes, yes. Sally, if you'll just move your books—*(He seats the CONSULTANT down at the table.)* You did say, last time, that the kitchen table was a good place for our ... our meetings?

CONSULTANT: There's nothing like getting your elbows together on a kitchen table. I'm a minute and a half late, I'm afraid. But nothing to fret or worry over—

FATHER: *(He slips into the living room and whispers.)* She's here.

MOTHER: Who's here?

FATHER: You know—her. That person. From the Fret-and-Worry Bureau. I completely forgot that today was our day.

MICHAEL: But didn't we just have our visit?

MOTHER: A month ago.

MICHAEL: Great timing, I'm halfway through the Scramble.

MOTHER: Can't be helped. Hurry now.

FATHER: *(To MICHAEL.)* On your feet, son. You can't keep these Fret-and-Worry people waiting.

> *(They assemble around the table, each knowing where to sit. Family members stare straight ahead while they speak and do not respond to what the others are saying, giving the proceedings the air of a one-to-one confession. As each person speaks, he or she puts on a sort of prayer shawl or scarf; MOTHER wears it first. The CONSULTANT takes notes.)*

MOTHER: *(Clearing her throat.)* Always first, it seems I always have to go first. Well ... on a part-time basis I worry about my teenage daughter who's always crying in her bedroom. She thinks I don't know, but it's like I'm cursed with x-ray vision, I can tell when she's crying. I worry about my son, too, who stands on his head a lot. That's something I've noticed, but so far I haven't said anything. I've got this sixth sense about everyone in this house, *(Angrily.)* everyone except me. *(Softening.)* How can that be? It's a mystery, and the mystery keeps getting deeper *(Angry.)* and deeper. *(Softer.)* I worry—this is an on-and-off worry—about Brian. I try to buy only healthy things but he somehow finds *(Angry.)* all the bad stuff. *(Softer.)* Also he blinks a lot. All the time. I worry because I spend so much time being nonchalant, *(Self-mocking.)* humming, singing, murmuring my motherly murmurs, keeping things light-hearted and casual, keeping trouble away. Nonchalance—it used to be a kind of girlish hobby with me, ha—*(Angry.)* but now it's like a full-time job. Sometimes I look up and I seem to see someone like me, but not exactly like me, standing with her arms spread out, trying to hold it—everything—all together. I hold the whole house together, *(Angry.)* the whole universe. Was this in the job description? Everyone expects me to be nonchalant, it's my only talent. I don't dare stop humming. *(Softening.)* I also worry about the window, the upstairs window. I worry even more about worrying about the window, how I can't stop thinking about it. I'm at a place in my life where I'm sick of my inner thoughts *(Angry.)* and my outer thoughts. And something else, sometimes, late at night when everyone's asleep, *(Angrily.)* except for me that is, *(Softening.)* I hear this dog barking. Most of the neighbours around here are pretty good about their dogs, keeping them quiet, I mean. But there's this one. I don't know who he belongs to, maybe no one. A stray dog. He'll start barking and he'll keep it up. Like he wants something, or someone, and whatever it is, he wants it just terribly.

CONSULTANT: We'll move on now, thank you.

> *(MICHAEL takes the shawl from MOTHER and puts it on. MOTHER, like the others, stares straight ahead.)*

MICHAEL: Well, I dunno, there's the usual worry, the same old one I mentioned last time. *(Laughs nervously.)* That I'm a little—ha!—crazy? You know? Insane? But I'm getting used to that one. It feels almost like normal now. But I've got this weird feeling ... that something's not quite right in this house, y'know? Something's not ... here. It's not finished, there's like a hole in the roof or something. The problem is I notice things that other people don't notice, it's like my eyes and ears are too sharp for my own good. Here's a for instance: I can hear my sister Sally crying at night. Only, I couldn't possibly hear something like that, could I? Not when my mom's got the TV turned up full blast and my dad's rattling things in the kitchen. And when he rattles things he rattles things *hard*. Like he'd like to kill all that stuff we've got in the cupboards. The plates and cups, the knives and forks, the pans, the pots, the oven door, you name it, he's rattling everything *to death!* He's like this terrible rock band that can't stop playing, like someone's put a magic spell on it, turned the key all the way, it's just going to go on playing forever and ever, and so loud it's covering up all the good healthy sounds. Like, like the snowplow going by at night. Dchchewvv. *(Lingers over this.)* Dchchewvv. I think of that guy out there all alone ... Dchchewvv. Clearing away the snow while the rest of the world is sleeping, he's like a hero, y'know. I love that sound. And then there's this dog I hear barking sometimes at night. I really like lying in bed and listening to that dog, it's like he's barking just for me. If I could bark I'd bark just like that. A big loud wild bark that says—it says everything. Like it doesn't leave one single thing out, it's the greatest. But the funny thing is, when I hear it, it makes me, sort of, want to cry.

(MOTHER passes the prayer shawl to SALLY.)

SALLY: I worry because I have this *hideous* affliction. I'm forced to do this impersonation *all the time* of this vacuous person who worries about zits and boyfriends and how my hair looks, and the truth is I'm worried about God and peace and humankind and the future of women in the national workforce. I'm falling behind too. My brain, I mean. Like, I've learned the solar system ten times already. The first time in grade three, then there was grade six with Mr. Neilson; he did the rotation of the earth and sun with a flashlight and an orange. God, it was beautiful—half the orange turning dark, half of it lit up golden-like. For about two seconds there I actually understood the whole concept of the cosmos, you know? Every year we do it again, I keep learning it and forgetting, learning and forgetting, and how am I going to be able to live in the world if I can't remember what goes around what, and how long it takes to—

CONSULTANT: *(Writing in her notebook.)* Just a minute now, hold on there, please. Is this particular concern a worry or a fret, would you say?

SALLY: That's the problem, *right there*. I've got like *zero* perspective. Mountain, molehill, it's all the same, and it's all sliding by me, like a television show. I'll grab hold of a brand new worry, I'll get all worked up, and I'll start to cry, and then it goes by, zooooom, like it doesn't even care if I'm fretting and worrying about it. Like this week, right now, I've got this huge, gigantic worry about the end of the world coming? The end of the world, and then, y'know, I go down to the mall and I see these people shuffling out of the garden centre with flats of marigolds that they've actually going to take home and plant in their poor stupid doomed gardens, for God's sake. I worry because I can't decide what my opinions are; if I'm going to grow up and be one of those women eating salads in cafeterias or if I'm going to get fat and go out to the library a lot and wear Rockports that don't go with my outfits but I don't care about that one little bit because they feel so nice and comfy on my feet. You probably won't believe this, but inside my brain I've got all these lovely, graceful ideas folded up, beautiful thoughts, unselfish thoughts, thoughtful thoughts, but when I open my mouth ... out comes this, this ... garbage. I'm like a poison pasta machine, I'm spewing out black, oily streams of ... worry. And at night, you know, I dream about this dog that's barking, it's just a bark, your regular standard neighbourhood dog bark, but this particular dog is, like, talking? Oh my God, it's awful what he's saying. He's saying *(Whispering in a tiny voice.)* help me, help me.

(Sally hands the prayer shawl to FATHER, and then stares straight ahead.)

FATHER: This house, these walls, these rooms. Maybe people aren't meant to live like this, in separate cubicles with doors between them that open and shut. Now if Sally and Michael and Jane and I moved to a nice big friendly *(Long pause.)* cave, maybe we wouldn't worry and fret so much about being ... lonely. Not that I'm lonely at this precise moment. I'm just getting ready to be lonely, I'm steeling myself, you might say, I'm in a sort of holding pattern at the moment. The kids are growing up, my daughter cries her eyes out, my son stands on his head, so what can I do? I see loneliness in the future; I see disappointments ahead. I feel we're on the verge of something. Sometimes I feel like I'm a squatter in this family, watching and waiting for "it" to happen. Whatever "it" is. Y'know, what I'd really like to be is one of those men with a twinkle in my eye. I've practised in the mirror a lot, but all I can do is ... blink. At my time of life I should be delving into the higher truths, the nature of the universe, good versus evil, but it's hard to concentrate. My ties are all mixed up, the wide ones and the narrow ones, the plains and the patterns, the stripes and the ... My golf clubs, my fishing tackle, everything's jumbled together. Something's been misplaced, something important, but I can't seem to concentrate on what it is. Forgetting is what I worry about, not remembering. Forgetting is what hurts. Also my wife. You know how most people turn the sound off on the TV and just leave the picture? Well, she does just the opposite. She turns the sound up as loud as it'll go and she sits there, just staring into that little grey blank screen like she's looking for something that's lost and gone forever. Something that can't be replaced. Part of her body. Or part of us. Another thing, real estate values are dropping, the neighbourhood's going to hell, stray cats and dogs running all over the place. There's this one dog that keeps everyone awake howling and barking, I keep meaning to phone the police or the dog catchers or whoever, but the days go by and I ... forget.

(The microwave dings. The CONSULTANT stands up, puts his/her notes in his/her bag, and pulls out a small parcel which she places in the middle of the table.)

CONSULTANT: Now here's your coping kit for this month. Or, no—*(She replaces the parcel and pulls out an identical one.)* that's for another family. Here's yours. Keep the frets in check and remember to update your worry charts, but don't be overly concerned about ... about anything. I'll see you in thirty-one days.

(The CONSULTANT exits. The family remains frozen at the table.)

FATHER: *(Clearing his throat and speaking.)* Well, that's over for another month. And now it's time—

MOTHER: *(Singing, holding note.)*
It's time.

MICHAEL: *(Singing, holding note.)*
It's time.

SALLY: *(Singing.)*
It's ti-i-i-me!

(They rise and spread out across the stage.)

ALL: *(Singing.)*
Time to climb on,
The worry-worry train,
All alone on the worry-worry train,
All aboooardddd.
All alone on the worry-worry train.

MOTHER:
Why can't we talk to each other?
Why can't we share our concern?

FATHER:
Mother, father, sister, brother,

Our troubles simmer and burn,
Our sorrows darken and die.

ALL:

And life goes by.
It's time, it's time, it's time,
It's time to hurry,
Time to hurry,
Gotta hurry up for
The worry-worry train.

SALLY:

All these thoughts that weigh me down,
All the things I keep inside.

MICHAEL *and* SALLY:

All the troubles we've got stored,
Could be lighter if we only shared.

ALL:

Allllll abooooard!
Time to climb on
The worry-worry train,
All alone on the worry-worry train.

Track one, track two, track three, track four,
It's time, it's time, it's time.
Hurry up for the worry-worry train,
All alone on the worry-worry train.

MOTHER *and* FATHER:

If we could get our problems
Off our chest,
Reduce our load of daily stress.
If you confessed, and you confessed,
And he confessed, and she confessed,
Then less would be more,
And more would be less.
Everyboooooody, everyboooody,
Hurry, hurry,
All aboard for the worry express.

ALL: North, south, east, west,
We're each alone on,
The worry-worry train.
All abbooooardd.

SALLY:
All the stuff that makes us blue.

MICHAEL:
Bottled up like crazy glue.

MOTHER *and* FATHER:
Down to the station,
Down to the station.
What became of communication?

ALL:
It's time, it's time, it's time,
Time for the worry-worry train,
All alone on the worry-worry train.

MOTHER:
If we could exorcise our miseries.

FATHER:
Dispel our small anxieties.

ALL:
Wash our troubles down the drain.
It's time, it's time, it's time,
All alone on the worry-worry train.

FATHER *and* MICHAEL:
All the cares that go unshared,
Keep us separate.

MICHAEL:
Keep us scared.

SALLY:
I'm scared.

MOTHER:
And I'm scared.

ALL:
Everyone's scared,
On the worry-worry train.
Solitude is fuel for grief,
And grief is food for solitude.
Secrecy contaminates.

FATHER:
Liberates?

MOTHER:
  Exaggerates.

ALL:
  So why can't we talk to each other,
  Why can't we share our concerns.
  Mother, father, sister, brother,
  Our troubles simmer and burn,
  Our sorrows darken and die,
  And life goes by.

  Grief and frenzy and despair,
  All they need is a little air.
  A little air and a little time,
  It's time, it's time, it's time, it's time,
  Time to climb on the worry-worry train,
  All alone on the worry-worry train.

  *(Part of song is repeated as lullaby, as the family withdraws for
  the night. MICHAEL and SALLY go to their beds; MOTHER
  and FATHER disappear into their bedroom. Darkness and
  silence falls over the house. The long lonely bark of a dog can
  be heard. Then MICHAEL sits up in bed, turns on a flashlight
  and comes downstairs through the kitchen, mimes opening the
  door to let a dog in. SALLY has also turned on a light; she
  descends, stoops and pats imaginary dog. Then MOTHER and
  FATHER arrive in the kitchen, observing the scene. MOTHER
  opens the fridge to get out some milk, and pours it into a bowl
  for the dog. FATHER rummages in a cupboard for Cheerios,
  putting a few on the floor for the dog. The family gathers
  around, making it clear that the dog has been welcomed. The
  lights fade.)*

Act Two

Scene One

(A dark stage with the set completely blacked out. An immense face, belonging to the POET, is projected on the floor. Loud hip-hop music plays under the monotone-but-ultra-hip voice of the POET. His voice is like a beat poet under water with run-on sentences that rise rather than fall at the ends.)

POET: *(Emphasising italicized words.)* Today I pressed my nose against a *mirror.* I could see better; *clearer.*

(FATHER comes down "runway," posing and turning.)

Here's our father. Righteous *function man.* Shoulders expand through *cloth.* Ready to listen—he's made *room.* He's done his time in the rethink tank. Authentic jeans have more *give.* He can stand or *sit.* A witness to *form.*

(MOTHER comes down runway, posing and turning.)

Mother forms her own seams; finishing things off—but not all at *once.* She can layer, taking up more *room.* Air fills the new spaces. She howls at the *moon,* she's got moon clothes straight from the summer sales. She can slow her rush *forward,* and her silhouette gives nothing *away.* Fashion secrets are at *work.*

(SALLY comes down runway, posing and turning.)

Giirrll, she's *here.* She's checked in. Trans-avant-garde screened on her *chest.* She's retro-fitted. Her industrial construction shows through—each line a *connector.* She can spell *kinetic.*

(MICHAEL comes down runway, posing and turning.)

He's holding *on-line.* His fabric is in questions; expressionist alternatives *surface.* His parameters expand at *will.* Humour him. He looks for patterns; he gets hard-edge *abstraction.* And now, *(Breaking mood slightly.)* now we eat.

38

(The face of the POET on the floor disappears. Lights pick up the family in various parts of the house.)

MOTHER: *(Tying on a fluffy hostess apron, she picks up the dinner gong as if to strike it but changes her mind and sets it down. She clears her throat and sings out softly:)* Mich-ael, Sal-ly, Bri-an! Family dinner time.

(They enter and take their places at the table.)

FATHER: *(With the feeling of great satisfaction.)* Well, well.

MICHAEL: Gosh, pot roast and gravy. And mashed potatoes.

SALLY: Goodness. Cherry cobbler. With real whipped cream.

FATHER: Home-made too.

SALLY: Home-made and from scratch, or I'll eat my cotton gym socks.

FATHER: *(Leaning back.)* Now that's what I call one great family meal.

MICHAEL: Yeah. How come?

FATHER: But just look at the time, everyone. That special rerun of *Road to Avonlea* comes on in three and a half minutes.

MOTHER: Not so fast, Brian. Have you forgotten …

FATHER: But *Anne of—*

MOTHER: *(Patiently explaining.)* It's time … it's time for the whole family to sit down together and play a board game.

SALLY: A what?

MOTHER: A board game. You know, Monopoly, Chinese checkers, Clue. And so on and so forth. All happy families play board games.

MICHAEL: Only happy families play board games.

ALL: *(After a pause.)* And so they did!

SALLY: Maybe we could sing around the piano instead. *Down by the Old Mill Stream, My Grandfather's Clock—*

FATHER: Charades anyone? I'll go first … Or we could talk in the living room and tune into—

MOTHER: I really appreciate all the input each and every one of you is putting in, let me make this perfectly clear. Your commitment thing, Michael, Sally, Brian, to family fashion values touches me where it counts, right here, it really does. But ask not what your family can do for you, ask what you can do along with your family, and so tonight—and I do believe this was democratically decided upon at our last meeting, correct me if I'm wrong—*(Firmly.)* tonight is Scrabble night.

FATHER: Right you are. I was only kidding about *Road to Avon*—

MICHAEL: *(Running up to the table.)* Here it is! Here's the Scrabble board. Here, let me open it. There! Now, here's the score pad and a freshly-sharpened pencil. Here's the box of Scrabble tiles which I've already shaken thoroughly. And here's the timer and, just in case, you never know, the dictionary. I'm pretty sure, at least I sure hope, that I've assembled everything we need tonight. Mom, Dad, Sally, we're ready to begin!

FATHER: Why don't you go first, Sally?

SALLY: Oh, no, I think Mom should go first.

FATHER: Great idea, Sally.

MOTHER: Are you sure—all of you—that you really want me to lead off?

FATHER, MICHAEL, *and* SALLY: Yes, yes.

MICHAEL: Sounds to me, Mom, like we've got a one hundred percent consensus going here.

MOTHER: Well, hmmm, let's see now. How about—I suppose I could put down—it only uses up three of these little letters—but I might as well, I don't want to hold up the game for the rest of you. *(She puts down the letters.)*

FATHER: Why, that's absolutely terrific.

MOTHER: F- U- N. Fun. It's not much, but it—

SALLY: Good thinking, Mom. You're really on the ball when it comes to strategy.

FATHER: And resourcefulness.

MICHAEL: And that gives you—wow, seven whole points. No, double points for going first.

SALLY: Your turn, Dad. I hope you can do as well as Mom just did.

FATHER: Well, maybe I could. Yes, I think I can, if it's all right with the rest of you. I don't want to take an unfair advantage, but I could add on to Mom's word—C-T-I-O-N.

MICHAEL: Fun-ction. Function. Hey, Dad, you're cooking tonight!

SALLY: You're really working together, the two of you, that's what I think. Like a team kind of thing? You know?

MOTHER: And just look, everyone, two double-letter scores. Sixteen whole points.

FATHER: And now, Sally, it's your turn to show us what you can do.

SALLY: I'll just never be able to compete with you two, Mom and Dad, but, hey, there is one thing I could do maybe, I could sort of take these two letters I've got on my rack, this little A and this little L, and just sort of … you know … add them on?

MOTHER: Function-al! Functional. That's shows quick thinking, Sally. Ingenuity and innovation, and everyone knows that that's the key to Scrabble success.

FATHER: And not only that, it seems as though—yes—look everyone. Sally's L has landed on the—

MICHAEL: The triple word score!

FATHER: Sixty points! Be sure you write down Sally's score, Michael.

MICHAEL: I've already got it down, right after Sally's name, sixty points. Congratulations are in order.

FATHER: I'll second that.

SALLY: Wow. Thanks, Michael, Dad.

FATHER: Okay, Michael. Now let's see where your tactical skills are going to take you tonight.

MICHAEL: I don't know, Mom, Dad, Sally. I just don't see any possibilities here for me at all. I'm afraid I'm going to have to pass.

MOTHER: Come on, Michael. Don't give up. I just know, with a little bit of persistence and effort, you can do it.

MICHAEL: Thanks a lot, Mom, for the encouragement. But, you see, I've got this Y on my rack. I was hoping for a couple of vowels but—

SALLY: Y's are the absolute worst. Well, except for Z's. That's too bad, Michael, getting stuck with a Y.

FATHER: It's not your fault, son. Getting a Y could happen to anyone.

MICHAEL: Of course, maybe I could—I don't know, but I could …

MOTHER: Go ahead, Michael. Don't hold back. Do what you have to do.

MICHAEL: Well I could take this D I've got and this Y, and stick this S in—

SALLY: And?

MICHAEL: And put all three letters in front of functional and I'd get—

MOTHER: Dys-functional.

MOTHER, FATHER, *and* SALLY: Dysfunctional? *(They roll their eyes.)*

SALLY: *(Sarcastically.)* What is it? Four o'clock? Oprah's on!!

MICHAEL: It's a real word.

SALLY: *(Sarcastically.)* Maybe we should dialogue about this new word.

MICHAEL: The Y's worth twelve points on its own, plus eight points for D and S, plus sixty points for the rest—

MOTHER: Look me in the eye, Michael. I want the truth. Where, and from whom, did you pick up this ... dys-functional.

FATHER: Those no-good friends he's always hanging around with. I told you—

SALLY: A bunch of dickheads.

FATHER: Sally!

SALLY: *(Overlapping with FATHER.)* You could be watching *Anne of Avon*—

MOTHER: I'm disappointed in all of you. What kind of a family is this! I thought when we got the Scrabble board out tonight, after pot roast and mashed potatoes, after home-made cherry cobbler and real whipped cream, that we were going to have a little ... fun.

FATHER: Exactly what I thought. Some family fun.

SALLY: So, Michael, why do you always have to go and spoil our fun?

MICHAEL: *(Pause.)* What is fun anyway? I mean, what is it. *(He pronounces the word "fun" in different ways, like a word in a foreign language.)* Fun. Fun. Fun? Fun! Fun. *Fun.* ... *(Sings.)* Fuuuun, funnnnnnnnn.

SALLY: *(Joining in song, running up and down scale.)*
Fun, fun, fun, fun, fun, fun ...

FATHER: *(Singing in* Pachelbel's Canon-*mode, not ironically, or exaggerated, but with beautiful phrasing and voices overlapping at some points.)* Fun, functional, fun, functional, I say fun-fun-functional—

MOTHER: *(Singing along.)*
More or less functional,
Occasionally functional,
Monday-to-Friday functional,
Fun, fun, fun-functional

ALL:
Functional family, functional family,
That's us!

FATHER:
We agree ...

MOTHER:
... most of the time.

SALLY:
Some of the time.

MICHAEL:
Occasional-ly.

ALL:
We're functional, fun, fun-functional,
Hitting on functional, that's our style.
Coming up functional, once in a while.
Once in a while, that's our style.
Fun, fun, functional,
That's us.

MICHAEL:
Dys, dys, dys...

SALLY: *(Overlapping.)*
... dys, dys, dys.

MOTHER: *(Overlapping.)*
... hiisssssss.

FATHER: *(Overlapping.)*
What's this, what's this?
What's this you're telling me? What's this?

MOTHER, SALLY, *and* MICHAEL:
Dysfunctional,
Dys, dys, dys-functional,
That's us.

FATHER: What do you mean dysfunctional? Haven't I provided for this intact family? Put my pay cheque straight into the family bank account? And another thing—

MOTHER, SALLY, *and* MICHAEL:
Dys, dys, dys-functional,
That's us!

FATHER: The real struggle is seeing how functional this family really is—

MOTHER, SALLY, *and* MICHAEL:
Dysfunctional, dys, dys, dys-functional—

MOTHER:
Who is it that puts a hot meal on this very intact table
Every single night?
And with moderate good cheer too.
Why, as a functioning mother, I've been just about ... perfect.
But, but, maybe, maybe that's not enough.
Maybe I've failed somehow, yes, yes, that's it.

FATHER, SALLY, *and* MICHAEL:
Dys, dys, dys-functional
Dys, dys, dys-functional.

SALLY: I mean, look at it this way, I could be a helluva lot worse than I am. It's not like I'm into ... shoplifting.

MOTHER, FATHER, *and* MICHAEL:
Dysfunctional, dysfunctional,
Dys, dys, dys-functional,
That's us.

MICHAEL: Look at me, hey. Just take a good look at me. I stand on my head and keep quiet and go along, what d'ya want anyway from a kid like me? Sometimes the only thing in the world I want is to get away from this family. And sometimes I can't seem to be here ... enough, you know? Anyway, I'm not old enough to be dysfunctional—

MOTHER, FATHER, *and* SALLY: *(Overlapping.)*

Dys, dys, dys-functional,
That's us.

FATHER: *(Holding the last note.)*
Like it's not as though we're into booze ...

MOTHER: *(Holding the last note.)*
Physical or psychological abuse ...

SALLY: *(Holding the last note.)*
Still, there are, if you look closely, certain clues ...

MICHAEL: *(Holding the last note.)*
I'm only a kid, I'm too young to lose ...

ALL:
We're dysfunctional, dys, dys, dys-functional,
We've got, we've got—

FATHER: What've we got?

MOTHER: Sing it out, sing it out—

ALL: *(Dancing.)*
We've got it,
We've reeeee-ally got it,
We've absolutely, poooositively got it,
Might as well admit it, we've got it, let's hear it, we've got it,
Have we e-ver got it,
We've got the dysfunctional,
Dys, dys, dys-functional b-lues.
Yeah!
The dysfunctional blues.

> *(They strike a pose at the end; the stage darkens. The only sound is a dog barking. They continue to speak to each other in the darkness.)*

MICHAEL: 'Night, Sally.

SALLY: 'Night, Michael. Good night, Mom.

MOTHER: 'Night, children. Good night, dear.

FATHER: 'Night, honey. Good night, children.

> *(A clock ticks as the darkness continues for a moment. MICHAEL turns on a flashlight, directs it around the room, then gets up and knocks on Sally's door. SALLY turns on her bedside lamp and sits up.)*

SALLY: Who's that?

MICHAEL: Me. Michael.

SALLY: What d'ya want? I'm sleeping.

MICHAEL: Can I come in?

SALLY: No. *(Sighing.)* Family, the real "F" word!

MICHAEL: *(He enters.)* Just for a sec.

SALLY: I'm in bed.

MICHAEL: *(Sits on her bed.)* I know.

SALLY: You're mucking up my Laura Ashley duvet cover—

MICHAEL: I'll be careful.

SALLY: You better be. What do you want anyway?

MICHAEL: I want to ask you something. It's ... important.

> *(MICHAEL and SALLY freeze as the light dims slightly. The light comes up in the kitchen. FATHER, in his dressing gown, opens the refrigerator and pokes around. He takes out a piece of cake and begins to eat it. MOTHER, also wearing a dressing gown, enters.)*

MOTHER: Can't sleep?

FATHER: You too?

MOTHER: Upset stomach?

FATHER: You want a sandwich?

MOTHER: You really hungry?

FATHER: Are you?

MOTHER: Or is it something else on your mind?

FATHER: I'm always eating, aren't I? Thinking too much.

MOTHER: So am I, I guess. And another thing, I hear that dog barking again at night.

FATHER: Sometimes two or three of them.

MOTHER: Those dogs, they're always going to be there, aren't they? Aren't they?

FATHER: *(Pause.)* What is it ... that wakes you up at night? Is it ... the same old thing?

MOTHER: *(Pause.)* Yes. The same old thing.

> *(They embrace each other and freeze as the lights dim and come up again in Sally's room.)*

SALLY: So what's so important you have to come barging into my private space in the middle of the night when I'm sound asleep.

MICHAEL: Were you really asleep?

SALLY: *(Pause.)* I was … almost.

MICHAEL: *(Conversationally.)* Hey, I haven't been in your room for a long time. Not in the middle of the night like this, kind of thing. So who's the guy? The picture on the wall?

SALLY: No one. *(Relenting.)* Elvis. That's his name, he can't help it. His parents liked the name.

MICHAEL: Is he the—No, he's not. He's the ice-skating guy.

SALLY: Look, you're supposed to be sleeping. That's what people do at night.

MICHAEL: Mom and Dad aren't sleeping. I can hear them down in the kitchen.

SALLY: Well, they have their separate … eating disorders to deal with.

MICHAEL: They do? Both of them?

SALLY: *(Mimicking Father's voice.)* Hey, let's make some popcorn. *(Mimicking Mother's voice.)* Okay, sweetie pie, eating's better than thinking, let's get those kernels dancing.

SALLY *and* MICHAEL: And so they did!

(They freeze; lights dim and come up again on the kitchen.)

MOTHER: Sometimes I think that if I can avert my attention from *it*, if I look not quite *at* it, there's a chance we'll all get by—

FATHER: And we'll stop thinking about *it*.

MOTHER: It's not so much that I'm thinking about it. It's not as organized as that. I'm just feeling it. It's pushing, pushing into me. And I still dream … about it … every … night.

FATHER: The window.

MOTHER: It comes back. I can't help it. I see the window standing there. Wide open. Do you? See it in your mind, I mean. I've never asked you before. But do you? Dream about it?

FATHER: It's worse in the day time. I'll be at work, and all of a sudden something will remind me. I hear that sound. And then—

MOTHER: And then?

FATHER: Then I hear … everything going quiet. It presses … down.

MOTHER: I know.

FATHER: And it goes on and on.

(They freeze, lights dim, and come up on Sally's bedroom.)

SALLY: You better believe it, he's up every night around this time. In the fridge, cake, ice cream, muffins, leftover salad, everything. His real life goes on inside that fridge, you know. Now Mom, she's probably making herself a sandwich. Basically, she's a more disciplined person than he is.

MICHAEL: So, how do you know all this?

SALLY: Someone has to keep track of things around here.

MICHAEL: I remember once, when I was little, I was scared there was an extraterrestrial in my room. Behind the door.

SALLY: Hey, it's late.

MICHAEL: I didn't want to wake up Mom and Dad about ... about the extraterrestrial ... you know? ... being there? So do you remember what I did?

SALLY: You shot him with your ray gun.

MICHAEL: I came in here. In your room. I woke you up. This was a long time ago. You really were asleep, I think, but you woke up. You let me ... get into your bed.

SALLY: What is this! An investigation into family incest? Give me a break.

(They freeze. Lights dim, and come up on the kitchen.)

MOTHER: Sometimes, sometimes I think you're right.

FATHER: About what?

MOTHER: About Michael and Sally. That we ought to tell them. You know. Everything.

FATHER: We've been over and over this.

MOTHER: It's just that I have this feeling—the way they look at me sometimes—that they suspect ... something. Something missing.

FATHER: It might be better for us all. If we did tell them, I mean.

MOTHER: I make up my mind that I'm going to do it. And then the next minute I think, they're just ... they're just children. If I can't bear it, how can they? And another thing—*(She stops herself.)*

FATHER: *(Prompting.)* Another thing?

MOTHER: I'm afraid, if we tell them, they'd never trust me again.

Never trust us. Why would ... anyone ... trust us? I don't even trust us. *(Pause.)* Do you trust me?

FATHER: *(After a long pause.)* Do you trust me?

(They freeze; lights dim and come up on Sally's bedroom.)

MICHAEL: What is incest exactly? What's it mean?

SALLY: Never mind. Forget about it.

MICHAEL: That other time? With the extraterrestrial behind my door? You let me get under the covers. You told me there wasn't anyone there, just a bunch of shadows. And then do you remember what you did?

SALLY: Look, I don't remember any of this. You're crazy, you know that?

MICHAEL: You showed me this warm place on the wall next to your bed. You put my hand on it. I think it's where the hot water pipe goes through. That's what you told me anyway.

SALLY: Hey, I remember that place. It's—*(She gropes behind the picture of Elvis.)* still here. Underneath Elvis.

MICHAEL: You told me how you always put your hand on that spot when you were scared at night. Remember, you used to be scared of the window ...

SALLY: It's just a window. For God's sake—

MICHAEL: And then you'd touch that warm spot on the wall and it ...

SALLY: It made the bad things go away. *(Gently.)* Yeah. Here, feel it, Michael. It's still here. Can you feel it?

MICHAEL: *(Puts his hand on the wall next to hers.)* Yeah.

SALLY: So, you said, when you came in here, you said you had something important to ask me.

MICHAEL: You know, I've been trying to kind of figure out how you get to be a person. You know? Like I'm waiting all the time for my life to start.

SALLY: *(Angrily.)* Michael, listen, you're already doing it; it's talking, and sleeping, and putting on your pajamas. This is it!

MICHAEL: Do you ever think, what I mean is, do you think that maybe there's something wrong?

SALLY: Wrong with what?

MICHAEL: Why don't we do things like other families. Hug, and kiss on both cheeks. And those feast days ... all that Folklorama stuff.

SALLY: Well, we have boiled eggs, and rootbeer floats on Friday nights. And we always go to the sugar bush every April.

MICHAEL: I guess. But, the way we are ... My friend Arnie, at his place, they just leave their bikes in the front hall. Just leaning there against the wallpaper.

SALLY: At Sue's? Everyone reads at the table. No one talks much, and they don't play Scrabble ever. And no one goes to work even.

MICHAEL: But our house—*(His voice breaks.)* Is it always going to be like ... this?

SALLY: *(After a long pause.)* Here, Michael, why don't you put your hand here again. On the wall. Next to mine.

(They freeze with their hands on the wall, lights dim. In the kitchen, MOTHER and FATHER hold hands across the table. The lights dim again and then blackout.)

Scene Two

(The sound of birds singing as the darkness yields to the brilliance of a sunny morning. MOTHER is upstairs polishing a window; MICHAEL is at the kitchen table eating cereal; SALLY is in the kitchen ironing a blouse; and FATHER is at front stage, bending over with hedge clippers. The birdsong grows louder while the family does a stretch and yawn. A NEWSPAPER CARRIER approaches FATHER quickly, breathing hard, and hands over the paper.)

NEWSPAPER CARRIER: *(Tripping over the curb.)* Hey, I'm kinda late this morning, sorry 'bout that.

FATHER: Not to worry, not to worry.

NEWSPAPER CARRIER: *(Panting.)* What happened was, I slept in.

FATHER: *(Happily.)* Well, it's Saturday morning. Why not sleep in? That's what Saturdays are for.

NEWSPAPER CARRIER: Some people on my route, maybe I'd better not say who, but their name begins with B, and they drive a big Buick, well, they get real bent out of shape when ...

FATHER: *(Looks up from his paper and pretends to see a neighbour.*

He calls out.) Hey, it's Bill and Betty Bentley! See you at the barbecue, Bill and Betty!

NEWSPAPER CARRIER: *(Calling in the same direction.)* I left it in the screen door, Mr. Bentley.

FATHER: Well, speaking personally, I can always wait for the paper. Just take a look. Murder. Epidemics. The education system. The economy. But along comes a morning like this, flowers coming up out of the ground, out of nowhere, the grass so bright and green and tender, and you say to yourself, who would believe we live in a troubled, misbegotten world.

NEWSPAPER CARRIER: *(Gesturing to the hedge.)* Hey, are you trying to cut that thing crooked? Like a modern art statement, or something?

> *(MICHAEL enters and FATHER hands over the coloured comics automatically. MICHAEL kneels down to read.)*

FATHER: *(Clipping.)* What I'm saying is, it's harder and harder to fall asleep at night, thinking of all the things wrong in the world.

NEWSPAPER CARRIER: Yeah, you guys sure messed things up.

FATHER: And then, this happens.

NEWSPAPER CARRIER: What happens?

FATHER: Look around. A fresh, crisp, brand new morning. The sun comes up. There's just the right velocity of breeze blowing through. And everyone, the whole family, awake and ready to—

NEWSPAPER CARRIER: I think there's something in the paper about a storm coming up.

FATHER: And you know the best part? It's Saturday! There's something special about Saturday. It's like we can put everything on hold, you know? And just look around. *(Seeing another neighbour, he calls out.)* Hey, Mrs. Sweeney, you were right about those numbers. Thanks! *(To the PAPER CARRIER.)* Just see the way the sunlight falls and rolls on that bush over there. A little miracle, yes it is. And take a deep breath. Go ahead, inhale. Now, doesn't that smell like a Saturday smell.

> *(NEWSPAPER CARRIER breathes deeply; MICHAEL, pained, sniffs the air, too.)*

On Saturday morning you forget your nightmares. You look around—*(He looks upstairs at MOTHER in the window, and then at SALLY in the kitchen and MICHAEL next to him.)* and well,

Saturdays save us somehow. They hold back the world for a little while. Saturday makes you feel you're in one of those old musicals and everyone all of a sudden bursts into song.

(The following song has an exaggerated 1940s big musical feel. MOTHER and FATHER sing from their spots in the house while FATHER and MICHAEL sing from the front of the stage.)

SALLY: *(Singing as she irons.)*
Saturday has a special
Wha'd'ya call it?
Kind of feel.
Like getting, I don't know,
A free five-course gourmet meal.

FATHER: Right on, Sally. And not only that.
(Sings.)
Saturday has a special, it's hard to describe ...
Look! I mean, Saturdays give you a break, let you off the hook.
If you know what I mean.

ALL: *(Singing.)*
There's something about a Saturday,
Something gentle, something kind,
You can take your time on a Saturday,
And let the day unwind.

Oh, there's nothing so winning,
As a Saturday morn-ing.
There's nothing so warming
As a Saturday morn-ing.

(Lights dim slightly, and a very faint roll of thunder is heard.)

SALLY:
Saturday irons the wrinkles out ...

MOTHER:
Saturday shines bright ...

FATHER:
Saturday is an all-day day ...

FATHER *and* MICHAEL: And then there's Saturday night. *(They give a high-five sign, as the faint sound of the* Hockey Night in Canada *theme can be heard in the background.)*

NEWSPAPER CARRIER: Saturday tastes like peppermint.

ALL:

It's filled with Saturday ways,
Saturday's like a birthday present,
Ev-ery se-ven days ...

(A flash of light suggests the onset of a storm.)

NEWSPAPER CARRIER: *(Speaking to MICHAEL, looking up at the house.)* You know something, your mother's going to wear a hole right through that window.

(Lightning, thunder, and the sound of rain drops as the NEWS-PAPER CARRIER hurries offstage. MICHAEL and FATHER run into the kitchen as the interior house lights go out.)

MICHAEL: Hey, the power's gone off. It's like—like night time.

SALLY: The iron. I have to wear this shirt tomorrow.

FATHER: And I was going to watch the golf tournament on TV.

MOTHER: *(Coming into the kitchen with a candle, she carries a photo album under her arm.)* Here!

MICHAEL: What's that?

MOTHER: A photo album. I thought, since it's raining outside, we might as well sit down and look through ...

SALLY: *(Sarcastically.)* My, my, what a cozy idea.

MOTHER: Please, children, sit down, I want to show you some of these old photos.

MICHAEL: Not those old photos again.

SALLY: We've seen them before. A million times. *(He crumples to the floor in total defeat.)*

MOTHER: Not these photos. You've never seen these.

FATHER: Honey, are you sure you want to—?

MOTHER: *(Her voice shakey but firm.)* Yes. Yes.

MOTHER: Now here I am, your mother, when I was, let's see now, about eighteen. You see, even prototypical nuclear families like us have their specific histories.

MICHAEL: Hey, black and white pictures. This was way, way back, right?

SALLY: What's that thing you're wearing, Mom? It looks like a, like a rug.

MOTHER: It's a poncho. Red and pink, if I remember right. With purple fringe.

MICHAEL: And who's that?

MOTHER: That's your father.

SALLY: Dad?

MICHAEL: Why's he ... why's he wearing ... beads ... around his neck? And that vest. Fringe! Cool. Do you still have that? I could ...

FATHER: No. It's gone.

MICHAEL: Aw! It's retro.

MOTHER: Now here we are at our wedding. You've seen some of these before—

SALLY: Neat dress. For that time, I mean.

MOTHER: And, look, this is what I ... wanted to show you. What I want you to—your father and me and—*(Her voice breaks.)*

SALLY: Is that me? Hey, was I ever cute, just the sweetest little— Hey, you look really happy, both of you, holding me up like that in that little sack thing. Like a magazine.

MICHAEL: Is that really you?

SALLY: *(Sentimentally.)* Yeah! What a doll face.

MOTHER: No.

SALLY: No what?

MOTHER: It isn't you.

SALLY: It's Michael?

MOTHER: It's your sister. *(After a long pause.)* Your older sister.

MICHAEL: Older sister.

SALLY: What—?

FATHER: She was ... beautiful, the most beautiful little thing, perfect. Little fingers, toes. Right from the beginning, these strong little legs kicking away. We couldn't believe—

MOTHER: We could not believe how lucky we were. She'd be asleep in her crib and we'd tiptoe in and just stand there, just looking at her. We'd sort of pat her from across the room.

SALLY: What is this? What are you guys talking about? Who is this baby?

MOTHER: *(Trying to be chatty.)* There she is on her first birthday. I made this terrible cake, in the shape of a teddy bear, vanilla and chocolate icing, it fell com-plete-ly to pieces when I tried to cut it, but, just look at her smile, she didn't care one little bit—

MICHAEL: I don't get it. I don't get what you're talking about. Who *is* this baby?

SALLY: What are you doing?

FATHER: Well, your mother's trying to explain—

MOTHER: She was ... she was your sister, before you two were even born or thought of, and she—

> *(Interior lights come back on suddenly, and MOTHER slams the photo album shut.)*

FATHER: The power's back.

MOTHER: *(She leaps up, reprieved but desperate.)* Yes.

SALLY: Wait a minute. I want to know—

MOTHER: *(Moving away.)* Never mind. It doesn't matter—

FATHER: You can't just—

MOTHER: Just forget I ever said anything. About anything. *(She tries to run into the living room, but MICHAEL stands in her way.)*

MICHAEL: *(Crying.)* I don't like this. This feels crazy.

MOTHER: Let me by, Michael.

MICHAEL: Not until you tell us what you're talking about ...

> *(MOTHER tries to leave again, but now FATHER stands in her way.)*

FATHER: Look, I know it's hard, but we've started and we have to go through with it—

> *(MOTHER tries to flee through the front of the stage, but SALLY stops her.)*

SALLY: *(Numbly, dazed.)* A baby sister. There was a little baby sister? Our sister! And she was older than me? What is this, some kind of riddle?

> *(MOTHER looks about desperately for a way to escape. She turns suddenly, opens the refrigerator door, and enters into it, shutting the door behind her. There is another flash of lightning and clap of thunder, and the lights turn off again.)*

Scene Three

MOTHER: *(In the darkness, she speaks from Sally's bedroom now.)* No! No, no, no, no, no.

> *(The lights come back on. MICHAEL, SALLY, and FATHER stand frozen in the kitchen. MOTHER stands upstairs by the French window which is now opened.)*

She was sound asleep, her afternoon nap. Oh, she was such an active little thing, she really needed that afternoon nap. She'd just go down without a word. Everyone said, what an angel! ... Oh my.

FATHER: Then, something must have wakened her up. A car going by, honking. Or else it was me. It was a Saturday, like today. I was cutting the grass, you see. At the far end of the yard. It could be she heard the sound of the mower, we had one of those old gasoline—

MOTHER: She got out of her crib. Climbed out. She'd never done that before.

FATHER: Never.

MOTHER: We had no idea she was capable of—

FATHER: She always had such strong little legs, right from the beginning she had these strong little—

MOTHER: The side was down, the side of the crib. She must have wanted to see what the noise was. She was always so curious. About everything that went on around her—

FATHER: So she came over to where the window was—

MOTHER: *(Proudly.)* She took her first steps at eleven months! Everyone said how—

FATHER: The window, it was ... open.

MOTHER: *(Touching the window.)* Opened.

FATHER: It was such a bright day. A hot day. Exceptional. It could be the sunlight made her a little dizzy—

MOTHER: And of course she'd just wakened up—

FATHER: I looked up and saw her up there, just this flash, her face, her little wisp of hair, she was swaying sort of—

MOTHER: She waved, remember, that's what you said afterwards, she saw you out at the far end of the yard and she—

(BABY CARRIER quietly enters carrying a rolled up blanket, pausing to listen.)

FATHER: She waved, yes, she waved to me, her little arm, hi Daddy, and then—

MOTHER: She must have lost her balance, she'd only been walking a few months—

FATHER: And she—she started to fall—

(BABY CARRIER drops blanket in a heap on the floor and then exits.)

FATHER: *(Rushing to the blanket, kneeling.)* My God, my God, my God. *(Looking up.)* What's happened. No, no, no—baby, baby.

MOTHER: *(Appearing by FATHER, kneeling with him by the blanket.)* Sweetheart, sweetie. Move your arms, say something, cry. Cry, oh please cry, say something.

FATHER: How did she—?

MOTHER: I don't know, I don't know. I went into her room and her crib was empty and then I saw the window was open and I—

FATHER: *(Accusingly, he shouts.)* You left the side of her crib down, I've told you a hundred times not to—

MOTHER: *(Hitting FATHER.)* The window. You left the window open, you knew there wasn't a screen on that window and you left it wide open—

FATHER: She never could have got out of the crib if the side hadn't been—

MOTHER: You killed her. *(Cradling the blanket.)* The window. A second story window, my baby, my baby, and you left it open and she just—

FATHER: It was such a hot day, she had to have some air, how could she breathe? I thought—

MOTHER: *(She hits him again.)* You killed her, you went and let it happen. You did it, you let it happen.

(MICHAEL and SALLY approach and the parents step aside. MICHAEL and SALLY stoop down, and then SALLY takes the blanket and rocks it in her arms like a baby. MOTHER and FATHER stand close by, side by side, but without touching.)

SALLY: There now, there, there now, hey, oh hey, what a beautiful little thing you are.

MICHAEL: Hey now, hey now. I always, I always liked ... babies.

SALLY: Shhhh, now don't cry, it's over now. It's okay. Shhh.

MICHAEL: *(Stroking the blanket.)* Don't be scared, that was pretty scary all right, but it's all over now.

> *(He turns and, seeing his parents, reaches for their hands. SALLY turns and sees them too. They draw MOTHER and FATHER together until the parents are standing behind the children. MICHAEL continues talking to the blanket, but also to all of them.)*

It's okay, it's okay, we've got you safe. We've got you now.

> *(FATHER and MICHAEL step out of the group as SALLY and MOTHER begin singing a ballad.)*

SALLY:
Mother, mother,
Why don't you hand me your troubles.
I've got a basket,
To carry them in.

MOTHER:
Daughter, my daughter,
Won't you please hand me your basket.
I've had my sorrows,
And heavy they've been.

MOTHER *and* SALLY:
These words, now spoken,
They'll lighten our burden.

SALLY:
You take one handle ...

MOTHER:
And I'll take the other.

Daughter, daughter,
I know your hands are willing.
But burdens this grievous,
Are not for the young.

SALLY:
Mother, Mother,
Give me more than your gladness.
I can share your smiles,

And carry your sadness.
Mother, mother.

MOTHER *and* SALLY:
These words now spoken,
They'll lighten our burden.

MOTHER:
I feel my heart,
Rising up from within.

> *(The lights dim to near darkness. The last part of this scene is performed in silence. The only sound is a flash camera. A flashbulb goes poof, briefly illuminating SALLY, holding the baby blanket, and MOTHER. FATHER and MICHAEL enter the second time the flash goes off. A third flash shows the complete family, this time in a slightly different pose. In the final flash, MICHAEL is holding the baby blanket in his arms. Darkness again.)*

Scene Four

> *(The lights come up on the living room where the family has gathered. The following scene has a tone of gaiety—the family is at its best.)*

FATHER: *(Pushing the couch.)* Come on. We need all hands on deck.

MICHAEL: We're moving the table? We've never moved the table before.

FATHER: Come on. Just two more feet.

MOTHER: That looks good. And now—bing! *(Idea!)*—The lamp table. Next to the rug. There.

SALLY: *(To the furniture.)* Hey, you two were meant for each other.

FATHER: *(To MICHAEL.)* Lamp! *(He runs off to get lamp.)*

MICHAEL: Hey, dust balls.

SALLY: You can add them to your collection, Michael. *(Considering the changes.)* It's off-balance. Definitely off-balance. But, you know, there's something kind of—

MOTHER: —Thrilling about an off-centre room?

MICHAEL: I like it. It's got the movers and shakers look. Hey, my basketball. *(He starts to dribble it.)*

FATHER: *(Removing a picture from the wall.)* Much brighter.

MOTHER: Why, it looks brand new.

FATHER: But not too new.

SALLY: It's just—different!

FATHER: *(Glancing at the TV.)* Look. Quiet everyone. It's coming on TV. The report on the nuclear family.

> *(They all sit and watch the TV screen flicker. The theme from W5 plays.)*

VOICE OVER: This evening, direct from the capital, we have the chairperson of the Royal Commission on the family. Our story tonight: "Family on the Faultline." *(More theme music.)*

FATHER: "Family on the Faultline."

SALLY: The faultline?

MICHAEL: *(Wearily, ready to explain.)* That means—

FATHER: *(Half-speaking, half-singing, he steps to front of the stage.)* Your fault—

MOTHER: *(Stepping.)* My fault?

FATHER: Our fault—

MOTHER: Their fault—

> *(They freeze. MICHAEL and SALLY step to the front of the stage, facing each other, and chant in rounds.)*

MICHAEL: His fault, her fault—

SALLY: Her fault, his fault.

MICHAEL: Our fault?

SALLY: Their fault.

> *(MAN TWO enters wearing a black derby, and carrying a lap top computer which he places on the kitchen table. The family sing the following, while MAN TWO interjects with comments.)*

ALL:
  Family at the fault line,
  Family at the fault line,
  Shaking, quaking,
  Sleeping, waking.
  Famil-ee-hee—

> *(They freeze as MAN TWO's watch alarm beeps. He turns it off and clears his throat.)*

MAN TWO: Time please. Please come to order. Is everyone present ready to review the transcripts of the family project to date?

ALL: *(Singing again.)* Family at the fault line, one, two—

MAN TWO: Order please!

MOTHER: All unhappy families are unhappy in the same way ...

FATHER: No, no, you've got it wrong, honey. All unhappy families are unhappy in different ways, or something or other—How does it go?

MAN TWO: Wait a minute, wait a minute. I'm trying to get this all down.

ALL: *(Singing again.)*
Family at the fault line,
My fault, your fault, our fault,
Family at the fault—

MICHAEL: A family is just a random scattering of genetic chips.

SALLY: A family is the basic building block of society and its most conserving agent. A family's whatever you want it to be.

MICHAEL: The trouble is, people are always trying to climb out of their families ... then falling back in—

SALLY: A family gives you your primary wounds.

ALL: *(Crooning.)* Fam-i-ly, fam-i-lee-hee—

MAN TWO: *(Speaking as he writes.)* A family gives you your primary wounds? Have I got that right? Can I quote you?

FATHER: A family is the crucible of ... of ... of ... I dunno—the crucible of ... hmmmm ... whatever. And another thing ... Now what was that other thing?

SALLY: Even an intact family can be pretty ... tacky.

MOTHER: Every tacky family is tacky in its own way.

ALL: *(Singing, clapping, including MAN TWO.)*
Family at the fault line,
Our fault, their fault,
One, two, three, four,
Salvation at the family door.
Family at the fault line—

FATHER: Now I remember what I was going to say. A family heals, protects its members—

SALLY: A family is like these people, you know? With nothing in common? Who sort of like live together, under the same roof kind of thing, even though—

ALL: *(Singing.)*
Family at the fault line,
Fitting in, fitting out,
Making up, making do.
Family at the fault line—

MOTHER: *(Speaking directly to MAN TWO.)* A family—I hope you're getting this down— helps you grow out of your silences—

FATHER: Or else freezes you in them.

MICHAEL: Families like to sit around and play ... y'know, games and stuff. Good games. And bad games.

FATHER: Talking to each other. Or not talking.

ALL: *(Crooning.)* Fam-i-ly. Fam-i-le-hee.

MOTHER: Families have a way of pretending everything is just fine, and sometimes—

SALLY: Sometimes it really is. Just fine. Oh, God, when that happens, it's heaven. It's like it's the only place you want to be.

FATHER: And ... I don't know why but, and this is what worries me, there're always these funny little pieces of family history that go ... missing.

MICHAEL: Maybe, sometimes, not all the time, but sometimes that's ... okay?

MAN TWO: *(Speaking as he types on keyboard.)* Hold on, I can't input that fast. I've got to get all this in the official report. You're saying that—

ALL: *(Singing.)*
Family on the fault line,
Their fault, our fault.
One, two, three, four,
Making up, making do,
Family on the fault line.

MAN TWO: What the sub-committee for the report for the Commission wants is—

MICHAEL: Wait a minute, wait a minute. I've got something to say.

MOTHER: Go ahead, no one's stopping you—

MICHAEL: You keep interrupting.

FATHER: Your turn, go ahead.

MICHAEL: I just want to say that a family—

ALL: *(Singing.)*
   Family on the fault line,
   Family on the fault line—

MOTHER: Shhhhh. Let this young person speak. Give him his moment.

MICHAEL: It's just that, well, with a family you have to take it or leave it, except you can't.

SALLY: Can't what?

MOTHER: Take it.

FATHER: *(Slight pause.)* Or leave it.

MAN TWO: The committee is expecting our conclusions today. Do we go with option A, B, or C, or all of the above.

FATHER: How 'bout none of the above.

SALLY: There doesn't seem to be any formula.

MICHAEL: Just say—

FATHER: Say we want to table it. Until the next century?

MOTHER: *(Hesitantly.)* We could, you know, just carry on and sort of see what happens-kind-of-thing?

MAN TWO: *(As he types.)* How's this? "In closing, we continue to watch, with interest—"

MOTHER: Eyes on the future …

SALLY: And the past …

MICHAEL: Let's remember to write it down—

SALLY: Listen! What's that noise?

   (A dog howls in the distance as the family freezes for a moment, listening, then carry on. After a long pause, they sing softly as the lights fade. Music has segued into gospel rhythm.)

ALL:
   Family on the fault line,
   One two three four,
   Trouble always at the door.
   Family on the fault line,
   On the fault line,

On the line, on the line,
Looking for a recipe.
Fami-l-ee, fami-l-ee.

Right there, right there,
On the line, on the line, on the line, line, line
Line, line, line, line, fault line,
Fam-i-leee-hee-heeee-ee.
Fam-i-lee-ee.
Carryin' on,
Carryin' on,
Carryiiiin' oooooonnn.

> *(Music and singing fades to silence as brilliant sunlight floods
> the stage. It slowly fades as a single dog barks. The end.)*